An Insider's Guide to
PAINTBALL

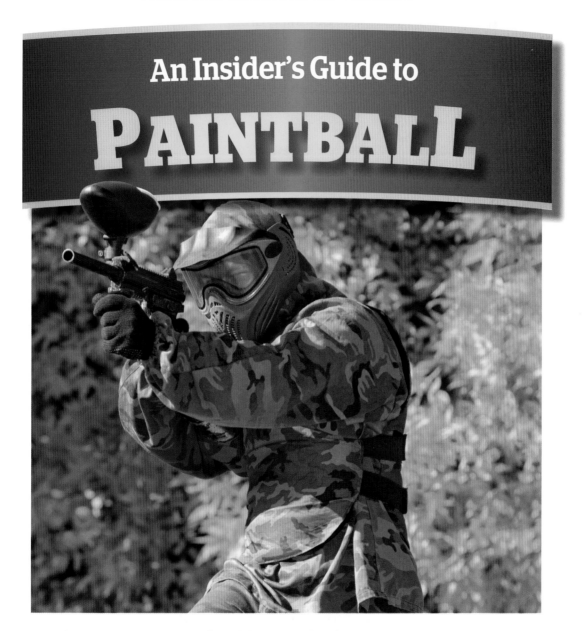

BOB POWER AND GREG ROZA

rosen publishing's
rosen central®

NEW YORK

Published in 2015 by The Rosen Publishing Group, Inc.
29 East 21st Street, New York, NY 10010

Library of Congress Cataloging-in-Publication Data

Power, Bob, 1959-
Sports tips, techniques, and strategies: an insider's guide to paintball/Bob Power and Greg Roza.
   pages cm
Includes bibliographical references and index.
ISBN 978-1-4777-8093-0 (library bound)
ISBN 978-1-4777-8094-7 (pbk.)
ISBN 978-1-4777-8095-4 (6-pack)
1. Paintball (Game)—Juvenile literature. I. Roza, Greg. II. Title.

GV1202.S87P68 2014
796.2—dc23

2014020355

Manufactured in Malaysia

Metric Conversion Chart			
1 inch	2.54 centimeters 25.4 millimeters	1 cup	250 milliliters
1 foot	30.48 centimeters	1 ounce	28 grams
1 yard	.914 meters	1 fluid ounce	30 milliliters
1 square foot	.093 square meters	1 teaspoon	5 milliliters
1 square mile	2.59 square kilometers	1 tablespoon	15 milliliters
1 ton	.907 metric tons	1 quart	.946 liters
1 pound	454 grams	355 degrees F	180 degrees C
1 mile	1.609 kilometers		

Contents

CHAPTER 1

Paintball: A History

Picture yourself hiding in the woods, alert for any movement around you. A gentle breeze blows through the branches above you. Your heart is still racing from the sprint through the woods, along the creek, and up the hill to your current position. You check yourself for paint splatter, but you are clean. As you try to plan your next move, you hear a twig snap nearby. Silently, motionlessly, you stay low and glance about. You know you have to move soon or you will be trapped.

Having strong survival instincts is a must in paintball.

Suddenly, a paintball explodes on the fallen tree right next to you! Wheeling around, you see two people in masks closing in on you. You hurdle the tree as more paintballs splat around you. The chase is on again. Your survival instincts tell you to duck behind the next tree and prepare to return fire. As you slide to a stop, a paintball explodes dangerously close to your leg, but you made it to cover. You quickly peek out and fire paintballs rapidly, catching one of your opponents squarely in the chest. "Out!" he yells. But you have little time to gloat, as a paintball splatters across your mask. "Out!" you yell reluctantly.

You leave the playing field with your opponent, laughing and talking about the chase through the woods. Hearts pounding and breathing rapidly, both of you are already looking forward to the next match. Next time, you think, I will survive and win...

The Game of Paintball

There are many exciting ways to play the relatively new sport of paintball. All of the different games involve "marking" other players with small, paint-filled capsules shot out of paintball "markers," or guns. The paintballs explode on impact, leaving a splotch of bright paint on a player's clothes.

A player who has been "marked," or hit by a paintball, is out of the game until the next round begins.

Keeping a 360-degree lookout for opponents is crucial to winning the game.

The markers used in paintball were originally developed in the early 1970s by an American company, Daisy Manufacturing. This is the same company that invented the BB gun in 1886. The first paintball markers were not intended for sport. Rather, they were designed for use in the forestry and cattle industries. Forestry workers used them to mark trees that were to be removed. They were also used by cattle workers to mark individual animals that had to be separated from the herd.

The Game of Survival

In the 1970s, two friends from New Hampshire—hunter and writer Charles Gaines and Wall Street stockbroker Hayes Noel—often found themselves arguing about human survival instincts. They had differing views on what it takes to survive when placed in a desperate situation, and they were both eager to test their survival skills in such a situation.

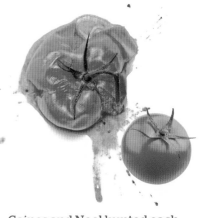

Gaines and Noel hunted each other with tomatoes at first!

They tried to come up with different ways to safely "hunt" each other in a natural setting, but they never developed a concrete plan. A few times they "hunted" each other through the woods with tomatoes!

Charles Gaines, shown carrying paintball ammunition, invented the game in the 1980s.

In the early 1980s, Gaines and Noel found a better way to evaluate their survivalist instincts. While reading an agricultural magazine, they discovered the paint markers that were designed to stain trees that had to be cut down. Instantly, the two men knew they had stumbled upon something big. They ordered two of the markers and tested them, discovering that they were powerful and accurate enough to use in a mock hunting situation. Equally important, they did not do serious damage to people. It wasn't long before they used the markers in a duel; Noel missed, but Gaines—the experienced hunter—hit his prey. After this short experiment, they began to push the boundaries of their survivalist instincts by stalking each other through the woods, each trying to mark the other before being marked himself. They named this game "Survival."

You need to be alert and stealthy while you go about collecting flags.

Gaines and Noel had help from a sporting goods dealer, Bob Gurnsey, in developing the rules for a large-group version of Survival. In June 1981, Gurnsey, Gaines, Noel, and nine other men from all over the country gathered in an eighty-acre area of woods in New Hampshire to play the new game. Each of them had a paintball marker, a pair of shop goggles, and a map of the area. Within the playing field were a referee and four stations set up with flags. The object of the game was to collect one flag from each station and return with the flags to the player's home base without being marked by another player. Any player who was hit with a paintball was eliminated from the game. During the two-and-a-half-hour competition, ten of the twelve players were eliminated from play. The winner of the game, local lumberjack and deer hunter Richard White, never even fired a paintball!

The Nel-Spot 007

Paintball markers were around for about a decade before the first paintball game was played. The first mass-marketed paintball marker was the Nel-Spot 007 (right), which was developed by Daisy Manufacturing for the Nelson Paint Company. The Nel-Spot 007 does not fire rounds. Instead, it fires specially designed paintballs, which are loaded into a magazine above the barrel.

(continued on page 8)

(continued from page 7)

The Nel-Spot 007 weighs about three pounds and is eleven inches long. It is powered by a 12-gram CO_2 cartridge, which is stored in the grip. Each cartridge can fire twenty to thirty paintballs before needing to be replaced.

Because it is reliable and accurate, the Nel-Spot 007 became the marker of choice for early paintball players. In fact, it was the type of marker used by all twelve players during the first paintball game, in 1981. For its importance in paintball history, the Nel-Spot 007 became famous in its own right. Thousands of paintball players continued to use the 007 into the 1990s, even as more advanced paintball markers were introduced.

Paintball Makes a Mark

One of the men invited to the first game of Survival was Bob Jones, a writer for *Sports Illustrated*, a popular sports magazine. He was given permission to write an article about the event. Gurnsey, Gaines, and Noel realized that once their

The Paintball World Championship takes place every year in Polk City, Florida.

The game has evolved a lot since the simple two-man game of Survival that Gaines and Noel played in the woods.

invention was published, a lot more people would be aware of and be able to enjoy this sport. They decided to call the young sport National Survival Game (NSG), which was also the name of their new company. Through NSG, they helped others set up paintball fields, and they made money by selling paintball markers and equipment. Initially, NSG made a considerable profit distributing paintball gear. However, once the word about paintball got out, it wasn't long before paintball franchises began springing up across the northeastern United States.

In 1982, two paintball fanatics from Chicago, Jeff Perlmutter and David Freeman, founded a company called Pursuit Marketing, Inc. (PMI). After unsuccessfully trying to work with NSG, Perlmutter and Freeman decided that they could market paintball themselves. Soon, people all over the country were ordering supplies from PMI. Most orders were from those who wanted to start their own Survival companies, and they often ordered thirty markers at a time. Interest in Survival exploded in the United States. Within a few years, NSG and PMI were not the only companies offering gear for this exciting new game.

Many newcomers to the sport did not want to spend hours wandering around eighty acres of woods. They wanted a quicker game with more action. As paintball became more popular, it transformed into a team sport different from the one-against-all competition that Noel and Gaines had invented.

Though Survival originally took place in the woods, most players now play paintball in specially constructed open fields.

In April 1982, Caleb Strong opened the first outdoor paintball field, in Rochester, New York. Other cities, including London, Ontario, soon had their own outdoor fields, too. The first National Survival Game Championship took place in 1983, in Grantham, New Hampshire. The winners were the Unknown Rebels from London, Ontario, and they won $3,000!

The first indoor paintball facility was opened in Buffalo, New York, in November 1984. Similar facilities began opening up in England, France, Germany, Spain, and Australia. Interest in paintball had erupted like a wildfire and spread to countries all over North America, South America, Europe, and Asia, as well as South Africa. Initially a male-only sport, paintball is now enjoyed by many women, too. Today, about 15 percent of paintball players are women.

Violence in the Game

It should come as no surprise that many people have objected to paintball, labeling it a violent game that simulates warfare and glamorizes guns. However, despite some similarities with military and law enforcement tactics, the sport is not especially violent. The attraction for many dedicated players is the opportunity to demonstrate superior survival skills.

According to Noel, paintball received unfair negative publicity in the early years due to its military look. The guns, camouflage, and goggles presented a violent image to those who were seeing the sport for the first time. It was hard for Noel and Gaines to make some people understand that violence was not what paintball was all about. To them, and to the majority of the sport's die-hard fans, paintball is about sportsmanship, creativity, fun, and being a team player. Most of all, the sport of paintball is about the desire to compete and survive under difficult and rapidly changing conditions.

Some critics are opposed to paintball because of its military overtone.

Professional Paintball

Most paintball players enjoy the sport as a weekend pastime. Some, however, have turned this weekend hobby into a professional activity. The International Paintball Players Association (IPPA), the first professional paintball league,

These Marines won second place at the
Marine West Coast Paintball Championship.

was established in 1988. In 1996, the IPA disbanded. Today, there are many pro and semipro leagues in the United States and Canada. The most notable of these leagues is the National Professional Paintball League (NPPL), which was established in 1992. Companies that make and sell paintball equipment often sponsor pro teams.

More than forty Marines participated in a game of paintball with their commanding officer
at Marine Corps Base Camp Pendleton in southern California.

There is also a college league, the National Collegiate Paintball Association (NCPA). Playing for a college paintball team can prepare you for playing professional paintball.

Pros earn money from sponsorships and endorsements, and some earn prize money for winning big tournaments. A few big-name paintball players have made money by starting their own paintball companies.

While most professional paintball players do not make much money, or any money at all, this could change as the sport grows in popularity. In early 2006, paintball superstar Oliver Lang accepted a $100,000 offer to

A sharp aim is critical to winning a paintball game. This player enjoys the game in Lublin, Poland.

leave the San Diego Dynasty to play for a team called the Ironmen, founded by the paintball retailer DYE Precision, Inc. This is the most endorsement money any paintball player has ever received. Most players feel this development proves that paintball is headed toward becoming a high-paying sport.

CHAPTER 2

Clothing and Equipment

You will probably need to spend between $100 and $200 on equipment before your first paintball match. However, you can usually rent equipment for less. Some sporting goods stores and online shops offer starter kits that cost between $80 and $100.

For your safety, you need to protect your whole body, like the player above.

The Equipment

Starter kits usually contain a marker, a hopper, one or two compressed air cartridges, goggles, a mask, and paintballs. More experienced players and tournament participants may want to purchase gloves, ankle protectors, uniforms, more expensive markers, and other accessories.

A complete paintball kit is essential if you want to start playing.

Markers

Paintball markers, also called paintball guns, launch paintballs using compressed air. Although there are several different systems, all markers work the same way. First, the marker must be cocked. This means the bolt is slid back so that a paintball falls into the barrel. A burst of air forces the paintball out of the marker through the open end of the barrel when the trigger is pulled. This happens every time you fire a paintball. There are several marker styles and brands, so you may want to try different kinds until you find the one you like best. There are three main types of firing systems used in paintball markers:

Pump-action. This is the simplest type of marker, perfect for beginners. Pump-action—or stock—markers need to be cocked every time you want to fire a paintball. They generally require small air tanks that can fire between fifteen and twenty-five paintballs before a new tank is needed.

Semiautomatic. The most commonly used type of firing system, semiautomatic markers need to be cocked only once, manually. After this, every time the trigger is pulled, the marker automatically slides the bolt back and loads a new paintball into the barrel, allowing for faster shooting. Some semiautomatic markers use compressed air to complete this process, while others use an electric motor.

Fully automatic. This style of marker continues to fire paintballs as long as the trigger is held down. Fully automatic markers are banned in many tournaments and leagues because they put players using semiautomatic markers at a disadvantage.

Air Tanks

To launch paintballs, markers need a propellant or compressed gas. The traditional option for compressed air is carbon dioxide (CO_2). Compressed nitrogen (NO_2) and high-pressure air (HPA) also have become popular forms of

propellant, although they are more expensive than CO_2. Propellant comes in a small aluminum cartridge that can be screwed directly onto the marker.

The compressed gas in the air tank propels the paintballs out of the marker.

Air tanks attach differently to paintball markers depending on their design. Some screw into the back end of the marker, and some attach to the bottom. Others attach beneath and parallel to the marker's barrel. The smallest tanks hold twelve grams of compressed air, last for about fifteen to twenty-five shots, and are disposable. Larger tanks can be refilled. The largest tanks contain twenty ounces of air and can fire one thousand paintballs without a refill.

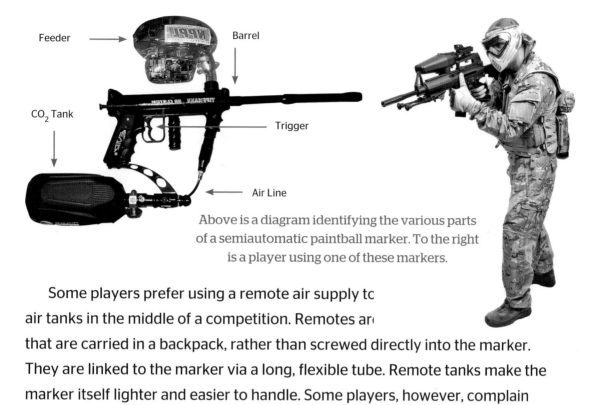

Feeder

Barrel

CO_2 Tank

Trigger

Air Line

Above is a diagram identifying the various parts of a semiautomatic paintball marker. To the right is a player using one of these markers.

Some players prefer using a remote air supply to air tanks in the middle of a competition. Remotes are that are carried in a backpack, rather than screwed directly into the marker. They are linked to the marker via a long, flexible tube. Remote tanks make the marker itself lighter and easier to handle. Some players, however, complain that the flexible tube gets nagged on branches or other obstructions.

The Paintballs

During a typical thirty-minute round of paintball, a player may fired dozens—perhaps hundreds—of paintballs. A paintball is a round capsule filled with paint, also called marking dye. Paintballs range from 0.50 inches to 0.72 inches, but the most common size is 0.68 inches. A paintball weighs only a few grams, not much heavier than a penny.

Paintballs come in all different colors and varieties.

The paint in the paintball is biodegradable, non-toxic, and water-soluble. It comes in a variety of bright colors, which helps in determining which player or team made a hit during a game.

Paintball capsules splatter on contact with the victim.

The outer covering of the paintball capsule is made of gelatin. This capsule is strong enough so that it does not rupture when being handled, but it is weak enough to break upon impact when fired from a marker. Upon bursting, the paintball leaves a mark that is about six inches in diameter. The farther a paintball travels, the slower it moves, and the greater the chance that it will not break on impact. Players should not try to reuse paintballs that don't break. The capsule may have been weakened, so the paintball has a greater chance of exploding while inside the barrel of the marker.

The Hoppers

A hopper is a storage container for paintballs. It is like an upside-down bottle that connects directly to the top of a marker and feeds paintballs into the marker one at a time. Standard hoppers use gravity to load paintballs into the marker. When a paintball is fired and the marker is empty, another paintball falls into place. Then the marker is ready to be fired again. Most hoppers available today can hold around two hundred paintballs.

Load your paintballs into the hopper, which will feed a paintball into the marker one at a time as you fire it.

Some players use motorized hoppers, which load the marker more quickly. Agitating hoppers have rotating parts that make the paintballs fall, rather than relying on gravity to do the work. Force-feed hoppers use a spring or another method to force the paintball into the marker. Motorized hoppers are quicker than gravity hoppers, but they also jam more frequently.

The Squeegees

On occasion, a paintball may explode while inside the barrel of a marker. This usually makes the marker unusable. For this reason, most paintball players carry squeegees with them onto the field. A squeegee is a long rod with a sponge or cloth

This player's specially designed harness helps him to carry around extra tanks and paintball containers.

attached to the end. It is thin enough to be inserted into the barrel. The sponge or cloth cleans paint from the inside of the barrel so that it can be used again.

Clothing and Safety Gear

It's important for all players to wear safe clothing from head to toe, like the player shown above.

Thick, protective clothing is a must when playing paintball. While it is generally considered a very safe sport, paintball does involve projectiles that can travel up to three hundred feet per second. These projectiles are not capable of piercing clothing. They can, however, cause a stinging sensation and even leave bruises. Because of these potential dangers, protective clothing is absolutely necessary. The most common attire is long pants, long shirts, helmets, masks, gloves, and goggles.

Protect Your Head

The most important pieces of equipment while playing paintball are the face mask and goggles. A flying paintball can seriously injure unprotected eyes and ears. Players are not allowed anywhere near the playing field without goggles and a face mask. Removing goggles during a game results in an instant ejection from the match. It is important to wear regulation paintball goggles, rather than ski goggles, lab goggles, or any other non-regulation eyewear. Regulation goggles can withstand being hit with a paintball traveling four hundred feet per second, fired from three feet away.

All protective face masks are well ventilated to enable comfortable breathing during heated competitions.

The Clothing

The type of shoes you wear depends on the terrain of the playing field. When playing on a grass or dirt field or on artificial turf, sneakers are usually best. Many players prefer to wear sports cleats for better traction. Boots are best when playing in a wooded area that may contain creeks, hills, and gullies. In general, the lighter the shoe, the more comfortable you'll be.

Uniforms and/or colored armbands are mandatory during regulation tournaments. During games that take place in wooded areas, many

Camouflage clothing helps players blend into their surroundings and escape notice.

players choose to wear camouflage. This provides an edge, though it is not compulsory. Players wearing camouflage blend into their surroundings better, increasing their chances of surviving the game.

Many experienced players choose to wear harnesses when playing paintball. A harness is an article of clothing that contains tight straps or loops designed to hold air cartridges, paintball containers, a squeegee, and sometimes a second marker. Some harnesses are slung over the shoulder or around the neck, others are worn like a belt, and the rest are secured tightly to arms and legs.

Paintball Markers and the Law

The federal government does not regulate paintball markers as it does actual firearms (guns). However, federal law does say that the use of a "look-alike" firearm in any criminal activity will result in the same penalties as if an actual firearm was used. It's also against federal law to board an airplane with containers of compressed air. If you must fly with your paintball equipment, never bring compressed air with you. Notify the airline before arriving at the airport, and secure all equipment in luggage that can be checked before getting on the plane.

You should always be aware of local laws regarding paintball markers and equipment. Local governments often have specific laws regarding their use, and some laws are stricter than others. You should also keep in mind that a paintball marker looks very much like a real firearm—especially with the hopper and air tanks removed. Carrying it in public places, such as a park or playground, is asking for trouble. Police officers may think you are carrying a real gun, and they would be justified in taking the steps necessary to detain you. Remember to carry your paintball marker in its case or bag.

CHAPTER 3

How to Play

There is no specific set of rules for paintball because so many variations of the game can be played. However, there are some rules common to all paintball games.

Typical Rules

The first rule of paintball is to keep your goggles on at all times. Being struck in the eye with a paintball can cause serious injuries, and even blindness. Sometimes, in the heat of a competition, goggles can become foggy, reducing a player's vision. Still, this is no reason to remove them. Any player caught without regulation protective eyewear in the "goggle zone" is immediately ejected from the competition.

Under no circumstances should you take off your safety goggles midway through a game.

Physical contact is not allowed during paintball. In fact, a player should not be within five feet of a player from another team. This rule is designed to prevent players from being hurt by paintballs fired at close range. When two opponents come within five feet of each other, one or both must move back before firing. Both players will be disqualified from the game if they do not obey the rule.

If a paintball breaks on your uniform, gear, or marker, you must immediately put your arms up and loudly declare "out" or "hit" and use the safest and shortest route to leave the field, even if it was fired by your own teammate. This lets others know that you are out of the current match. If two players mark each other at the same time, both must leave the field. If you are struck by a paintball that does not break, you may continue playing. Once you call yourself out, it is against the rules for others to keep firing at you.

This player has been hit on his goggles. He must now put his gear down and declare himself "out."

If you are unsure whether you have been hit, ask for a paint check. Opponents cannot try to mark you while you are being paint-checked. If the referee sees that you have been marked, he or she will call you out. (Usually the mark must be at least the size of a U.S. quarter.) If you have not been marked, the referee will announce that you are still in the game. When you declare yourself out, you must leave the field whether you were hit or not. If you are unsure, don't call yourself out until you get a paint check.

General Tactics

Though each variation of paintball demands specific strategies, there are certain general tactics that are beneficial to all players. One of the most important tactics of paintball is to keep moving. Rule number one is not to sit in the same spot for too long. Staying stationary allows other players to sneak up on you. Besides, most variations of paintball require a team or player to achieve an objective, such as capturing a flag. You can't do this by sitting in one place the entire game.

If you are unsuccessful at hitting a player who is hiding behind a wall or bunker, do not keep firing paintballs from your current position. Instead, think creatively and quickly. Changing position may give you a new view of your opponents, and it will keep them guessing what you will do next.

Sometimes it is necessary to rush at another player who has "bunkered down" behind an obstruction. This is a dangerous move because it puts you out in the open. However, by rushing forward, you often create a diversion for other players on your team. This allows them to move forward and possibly take out the opponent. Generally, aggressive players excel at this sport.

Depending on team strategy, paintball teams may either move together in a large group or split and tackle their opponents.

It is just as important to keep your eyes constantly moving as it is to keep your body moving. Never focus on just one target or area of the playing field. When moving forward, don't forget to look left and right—and even behind you. By remaining alert, you increase your chances of staying in the game.

Above all, remember that paintball is a game of survival. The better players are creative in finding ways to win, even when stuck in tough situations. For example, if you run out of paintballs, don't give up. You can still be useful to your team by drawing the opponents away from your teammates who still have enough paintballs to finish the game.

No Cheating

All regulation paintball competitions feature at least one referee to make sure everyone plays fairly. However, referees cannot be everywhere and see everything that occurs during a match, especially on large outdoor fields. This gives dishonest players opportunities to cheat. Some may try to wipe paint off of their uniforms after being hit. Others may set their markers to fire paintballs faster or more frequently than regulations

The referee checks this player's uniform for paint during the match.

allow. Most serious paintball players pride themselves on playing fairly. To them, if you can't win while playing by the rules, you don't have what it takes to be a paintball survivalist. Good paintball players respect other players and always play fair.

Variations of Paintball

Noel and Gaines' original idea of paintball was a one-against-all type of survival game. Once paintball caught on, however, team play became more popular. Today, people play numerous game variations. Listed in this section are just a few of the more popular ones.

Capture the Flag

Capture the flag is usually played by two teams on a medium- to large-sized field with a variety of natural or man-made obstructions. Each team has a base and a flag. The team that steals the other's flag and returns it to their home base without getting marked wins.

This player is jubilant after stealing the other team's flag.

Teams have offensive and defensive players during capture the flag. The offensive players quickly move out and try to take the other team's flag. The defensive players protect their own flag from being swiped. Team captains organize their players and give orders.

In a variation of capture the flag called center-flag, both teams must try to steal the same flag. As the name suggests, the center-flag is positioned in the center of the field. The team that steals the flag and returns it to their base first is the winner.

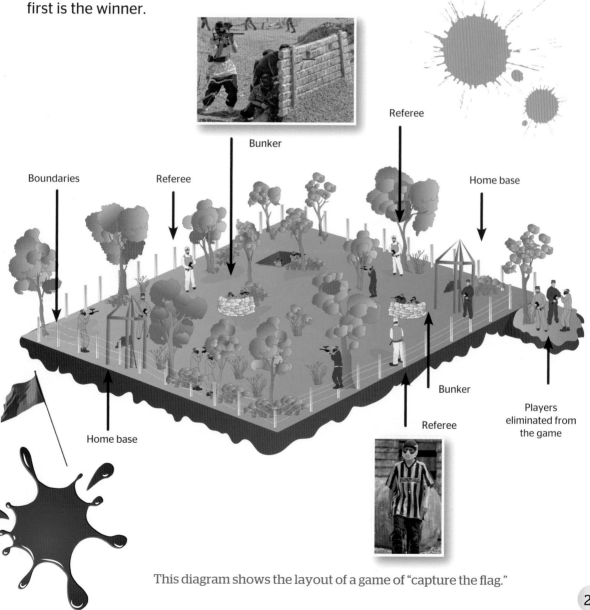

Referee

Bunker

Boundaries

Referee

Home base

Home base

Bunker

Referee

Players eliminated from the game

This diagram shows the layout of a game of "capture the flag."

Total Elimination

The object of the game is to mark all the opposing players from the match, thereby eliminating them. This variation is usually played on a small- or medium-sized field with man-made obstructions.

Players often sneak up on each other, which is why it is important to keep a watch out not only ahead, but also behind.

Total elimination is usually played with two teams, but it can also be played with a one-against-all format. This game is sometimes called speedball because of the fast pace of the game.

Scenario

Matches that follow a given set of circumstances are called scenario games. These are usually held on medium or large outdoor fields. Some groups meet to reenact historic battles. Others play through generic situations, like in a variation called supply chain. During this scenario, one team has to transport cargo (for instance, three portable coolers filled with fake supplies) from one point to another, while the other team attempts to steal that cargo.

Scenario matches often last from six to eight hours, and some last for a full twenty-four hours. Hundreds of players attend some scenario gatherings. These often end in a dramatic battle.

This referee cleans the bunkers while the teams wait for the game to begin.

X Ball

In X ball, there is a flag placed at the center of the field, which two teams of five are racing to swipe. A team is awarded a point for "hanging the flag" in their base. Once a team hangs the flag, they are awarded a point, and both teams take a three-minute timeout. When the next round begins, five players from each team return to the field. They can be the same five who were on the field for the previous round, or they can be new players. The team that hangs the flag the most during two twenty-minute halves is declared the winner. Similar to hockey, players who break the rules in X ball must sit in a penalty box for a few minutes before rejoining play.

Player Positions

The types of paintball players vary depending on the kind of game being played. Sometimes players are referred to by the position they take on the field, such as front middle or back left. In flag games, the person with the flag is called the flag runner. Or you may refer to players based on their job, such as defense or offense.

A sniper is a player who takes up a hidden position and tries to hit opponents without being seen. Snipers are helpful when the element of surprise is a must. They are perfect for defending a base against unsuspecting attackers.

Some players excel at bunkering. At the beginning of most paintball matches, it is essential to rush forward and control as much of the field as possible by hiding behind an obstruction or bunker and marking anyone who comes out into the open. To take out someone who is controlling a bunker, you must rush forward and put yourself at risk. However, allowing an opponent to bunker unchallenged can cost you the game.

Every team has a captain. Captains speak with the referees before and after the game to receive information and scores. They help keep a team organized and focused on the mission. College and pro teams also have coaches who yell out information to players during a game.

By hiding behind this bunker, the player is protected and can easily mark nearby opponents.

CHAPTER 4

How to Get Involved

Starting to play paintball is not difficult. The first step is to purchase the necessary equipment. Paintball gear can be bought at large sporting goods stores, at smaller shops that specialize in paintball equipment, and from online

distributors. Once you have your equipment, you need to learn how to use and care for it properly. Most store and field owners will show you how to use, maintain, and protect your gear. Habitual players often prefer to have their own

You don't need very flashy equipment to play paintball.

equipment. But if you are just starting out, many fields will supply you with everything you need for an afternoon of paintball. A trial run may help you decide if you like the sport.

Once you have the gear, you need somewhere to play. Many cities in the United States now have one or more paintball facilities in or just outside of the city limits. Larger outdoor fields can also be found in more secluded areas, miles away from cities. Both indoor and outdoor arenas continue to spring up all over the country, most of them featuring their own paintball shops. Fields usually charge about $30 per person and require that you use paintballs purchased from their shop. Though insured fields have some age restrictions based on local laws, private fields do not.

Even inexperienced players quickly realize that staying low to the ground is a good strategy to avoid getting marked.

Next, you need to find others with a shared interest in paintball. Often this is as easy as convincing three or four friends to purchase or rent the necessary equipment and join you. There are also hundreds of local paintball associations and Internet forums for people interested in the sport. These resources help players meet and plan competitions and get-togethers. Some groups of friends prefer to stage their own paintball outings in forests or fields on private property. Keep in mind, however, that you should still follow the same rules and safety guidelines that regulation fields enforce to avoid arguments and injuries.

Each time you play paintball, you will improve your skills and tactics. You will get better at bunkering, charging your opponent, and avoiding paintballs fired by other players. Experienced players are very creative and are constantly thinking of new ways to get the better of their opponents.

Playing Safe

Paintball is often perceived as a violent sport that involves hurting others. This simply isn't true. Physical contact between players is strictly forbidden. As with all organized sports, paintball is just a game and isn't worth fighting over. When you follow the rules and prepare for your own safety and the safety of others, paintball is an exciting, harmless, and friendly activity.

Dressing the Part

Paintballs can bruise and even break bare skin when they're fired at a very close range. This is why regulation play requires players to be at least five feet apart. At this distance, a hit may sting (depending on the amount of protective clothing you are wearing) but should not bruise or break the skin.

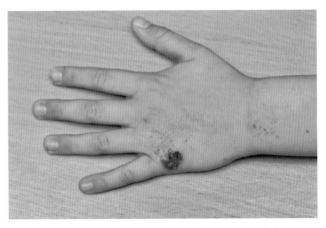

Always be sure to wear safety gloves while playing paintball, because getting hit on exposed skin can lead to a nasty blister, like this one.

While being hit with a paintball can hurt, protective clothing will prevent any real harm. The clothes you wear while playing paintball should completely cover your skin. Although it is best to wear old clothes, avoid any with holes or rips that may expose your skin. Thicker clothes will provide a cushion against paintball impacts. If it is a cold day, you should wear heavy clothing, as paintball players commonly spend up to six hours outside.

While old clothing is usually the best choice, worn-out sneakers or boots may increase the risk of slipping and injuring yourself. You may want to purchase appropriate shoes to wear on the field. Plan for the terrain and conditions. Wear boots with good ankle support to avoid sprains if you are playing out in the woods.

This player is wearing cleats to help improve his grip on the grassy field.

Ensure that you are wearing goggles, a mask, and a helmet that is designed for paintball. Never remove your goggles while on the playing field, even if they fog up, and never play with cracked or damaged goggles. Never fire your marker at someone who isn't wearing the proper equipment, especially goggles and a mask.

Other articles of protective clothing that you may want to consider include gloves, a hat, and neck protection—in other words, anything that will cover your skin. Some players also choose to wear chest and ankle protectors, knee and elbow pads, and cups (for male players).

Safe Use of Markers

Before a regulation match, all markers are outfitted with a chronograph to measure paintball speed. Each marker is set to fire paintballs at a top speed of three hundred feet per second. Higher speeds could possibly damage safety gear and increase the potential for injuries and accidents. Indoor paintball facilities often set the top speed at 270 feet per second because of the smaller playing area.

You must only remove goggles before or after the game.

Players should either engage the trigger safety on their markers or remove the air supply when they are not on the field. This helps ensure that people won't accidentally get shot. In addition, players must have a barrel plug in the end of their markers. Engaging the safety and using a barrel plug make it okay for players to remove goggles and other protective gear when they are off the field.

Gear Care

Always take care of your equipment and make sure it works properly. You should never look down the barrel to see if it is loaded or jammed. Never try to fire anything but approved paintballs from your marker. When not on the playing field, keep a barrel plug in the end of your marker to avoid accidents. Never leave your marker or paintballs in the sun, as excessive heat can cause the gas inside CO_2 and NO_2 cartridges to expand and possibly explode. Remove the air cartridge from your marker when you are not using it.

Unless you are trained to repair air guns, you should never attempt to repair a broken marker. However, for routine maintenance, most experienced players like to clean their own markers. This allows the marker to keep firing smoothly. If you do your own maintenance, make sure you understand how to take a marker apart and put it back together again. Books with step-by-step instructions on how to take apart, clean, and reassemble markers are available in stores and on websites.

Promoting Safety

Paintball manufacturers and governing bodies—such as the National Professional Paintball League (NPPL)—are constantly looking for ways to improve the equipment and the rules. In the years since the origin of paintball, key rule changes have helped to make it a remarkably safe activity. As with any sport, injuries are inevitable, but they can be reduced even further with relevant equipment and rule modifications.

These players rush into the field at the start
of the NPPL championship.

Mandated safety changes that have occurred in professional paintball over the years include stronger goggles, the use of full face masks, and harsher punishment for breaking the rules. In 2005, the NPPL changed its official rulebook to include a twelve-game suspension for any player who sets a marker to fire more than one paintball per trigger pull. This rule was designed to make the game safer for everyone and to ensure that no player was at a disadvantage.

Paintball in the Future

In its first year of business (1982), Pursuit Marketing Inc., the first major paintball equipment supplier, sold between seven thousand and eight thousand markers. This was far more than the owners had ever hoped to sell. It takes most new businesses two or three years to turn a profit, but within six

Paintball is spreading like wildfire all over the world. The South African Regional Paintball League (SARPL) (above) holds events throughout the year.

months of opening, Pursuit Marketing was making a profit. Obviously, paintball was quite the rage from the beginning, and its popularity has only grown ever since.

The U.S. Census Bureau reported that 5.6 million Americans participated in paintball at least once during the year 2001, according to a survey done

by the National Sporting Goods Association. Since then, paintball has gained even more players. The 2009 Census report indicated that 6.3 million people had played paintball that year. Other surveys have shown that paintball does not cause very many injuries. Paintball led to the fewest injuries out of the one hundred sports reviewed by the Sporting Goods and Manufacturers Association in 2001.

New technology and playing styles guarantee that people will continue to flock to paintball. In 2006, paintball retailers made about $434 million from the sale of paintball equipment worldwide. With numbers like these, it is obvious that paintball is a fast-growing sport. Now that you know how to get started, you can enjoy this exciting and challenging game of strategy.

Glossary

aggressive Characterized by high energy, quick actions, and an urge to attack first.

biodegradable Capable of being broken down by microorganisms into elements that won't harm the environment.

bunker An obstruction behind which a paintball player can hide and shoot at other players.

camouflage Clothing or devices designed to conceal the user by imitating the colors and textures of the surroundings.

cartridge A small, sealed case used to load a substance into something, such as compressed air in a paintball marker.

chronograph An electronic device that measures the speed of a paintball as it leaves the barrel of a marker.

compressed Squeezed or made smaller.

disband To break up.

disposable Designed to be thrown away after use.

eject To remove a player from a competition for breaking the rules.

enforce To make sure people follow the rules or laws.

erupt To break out suddenly and dramatically.

excessive More than necessary.

fanatics People who are extremely enthusiastic or eager about something.

forbidden Something that is not allowed.

gelatin A plastic-like natural substance that is used to make paintball capsules.

gloat To take pleasure in.

hurdle An obstacle or something that comes in the way of attaining a goal.

inevitable Something that is certain to happen and can't be avoided.

projectile An object that can be thrown, fired, or launched.

propellant A compressed gas that can be used to launch an object, such as a paintball.

regulation Approved for use, or conforming to guidelines set up by an officially recognized governing body.

rupture To break or burst suddenly.

secluded Describing a place that is not seen or visited by many people.

simulate To take on the appearance of.

squeegee A device carried by paintball players that is used to clean their markers.

superior Better than the rest.

survivalist Someone who is determined to stay alive or stay in a game by relying on his or her instincts and knowledge of the surroundings.

suspension The temporary removal of a player from a team as punishment for breaking the rules.

terrain The general physical features of a piece of land.

water-soluble Capable of being washed away with water.

For More Information

Organizations

American Paintball Players Association (APPA)

530 E. South Avenue

Chippewa Falls, WI 54729

(612) 605-8323

Website: http://www.paintball-players.org/

National Collegiate Paintball Association (NCPA)

530 E. South Avenue

Chippewa Falls, WI 54729

(612) 605-8323

Website: http://www.college-paintball.com

National Professional Paintball League, Inc. (NPPL)

15552 Graham Street

Huntington Beach, CA 92649

(714) 758-5575

Website: http://www.nppl.com

Magazines

Paintball 3X Magazine
570 Mantua Boulevard
Sewell, NJ 08080
(888) 834-6026
Website: http://www.paintballx3.com

Websites

Due to the changing nature of Internet links, Rosen Publishing has developed an online list of websites related to the subject of this book. This site is updated regularly. Please use this link to access the list:

http://www.rosenlinks.com/scc/paint

For Further Reading

Braun, Jerry, and Rob Rubin. *The Complete Guide to Paintball.* 4th ed. New York, NY: Hatherleigh Press, 2007.

Dell, Pamela. *Paintball for Fun!* New York, NY: Compass Point Books, 2008.

Grubish, Don. *Advanced Scenario Paintball.* New Brighton, MN: Modern Press, 2007.

Icon Group International. *Paintball: Webster's Timeline History, 1980–2007.* San Diego, CA: ICON Group International, Inc., 2009.

Larson, Christopher E. *Paintball and Airsoft Battle Tactics.* St. Paul, MN: Voyageur Press, 2008.

Multamaki, Martin. *Bunker'd!: Tournament Paintball Complete.* Bloomington, IN: Trafford Publishing, 2008.

Norman, Dave. *501 Paintball Trips, Tricks, and Tactics.* Mustang, OK: Tate Publishing & Enterprises, 2008.

Wendorf, Anne. *Paintball* (Torque: Action Sports). New York, NY: Children's Press, 2008.

Bibliography

Barnes, Bill. *Paintball! Strategies and Tactics*. Memphis, TN: Mustang Publishing, 1993.

Braun, Jerry, et. al. *The Complete Guide to Paintball*. Long Island City, NY: Hatherleigh Press, 2003.

EnjoyTurkey.com. "Basic Rules of Paintball." Retrieved July 1, 2014 (http://www.enjoyturkey.com/Tours/Interest/Rules.htm).

EnjoyTurkey.com. "What Is Paintball?" Retrieved July 1, 2014 (http://www.enjoyturkey.com/Tours/Interest/Equipment.htm).

Khan, Sami. "Tips for Beginners." *The Paintball Times*, February 1993. Retrieved July 1, 2014 (http://www.paintballtimes.com/Article.asp?ID=9).

Kloehn, Paul. "What Is the History of Paintball?" World and Regional Paintball Information Guide. Retrieved July 1, 2014 (http://www.warpig.com/paintball/newbie/rspfaq.shtml#history).

Little, John R., and Curtis F. Wong, eds. *Ultimate Guide to Paintball*. Burbank, CA: CFW Enterprises, 2001.

National Professional Paintball League, Inc. "2012 Official Rulebook." Retrieved July 1, 2014 (http://nppl.com/wp-content/uploads/2013/03/NPPLRulebook2012.pdf).

Sapp, Rick. *Paintball Digest.* Iola, WI: Krause Publications, 2004.

U.S. Census Bureau. "Participation in Selected Sports Activities: 2009." Statistical Abstract of the United States, 2012. Retrieved July 1, 2014 (http://www.census.gov/prod/2011pubs/12statab/arts.pdf).

Index

About the Authors

Greg Roza is a writer and editor specializing in library books and educational materials. He lives in Hamburg, New York, with his wife, Abigail, his daughter, Autumn, and his son, Lincoln. Roza has a master's degree in English from SUNY Fredonia, and he loves to stay in shape by participating in outdoor activities.

Bob Power is an author and editor who grew up exploring the woods of central New Jersey. He now lives on Long Island, but remains an enthusiast of outdoor activities.